BLOOD
MOUNTAIN

BLOOD
MOUNTAIN
JOHN ENGELS

University of Pittsburgh Press

Published by the University of Pittsburgh Press, Pittsburgh, Pa. 15260
Copyright © 1977, John Engels
Feffer and Simons, Inc., London
Manufactured in the United States of America

Library of Congress Cataloging in Publication Data

Engels, John.
  Blood Mountain.

  (Pitt poetry series)
  I. Title
PS3555.N42B6   811'.5'4   76-26854
ISBN 0-8229-3338-1
ISBN 0-8229-5277-7 pbk.
ISBN 0-8229-3289-X spec. binding

Acknowledgment is made to the following publications for permission to re-
print poems that appear in this book: *The Hollins Critic, Poetry Northwest,
Poetry Now, Prairie Schooner,* and *The Virginia Quarterly Review.*

Some of the "Blood Mountain Poems" included in this volume were originally
published in the *Carleton Miscellany,* Vol. XVI, No. 1–2 (Double Issue) and
are reprinted with permission of its editor.

"A May Snowstorm" was first published in the *Sewanee Review* 83 (winter
1975) in a different version. Copyright 1975 by the University of the South.
Reprinted by permission of the editor.

It is how I try to tell you
There are no imbalances: we stand
At whatever center most
employs us.

CONTENTS

A May Snowstorm   3

A Dream with Furtwängler in It   6

West Topsham   9

Falling on Blood Mountain   14

Waiting for Kohoutek   15

Vertigo on Blood Mountain   17

Early Morning Poem   18

Bad Weather on Blood Mountain   21

The Fire   23

Toutes les lumières   25

At the Top of Blood Mountain   27

The Intruder   29

Photograph When You Are Not Looking   31

Dawn on Blood Mountain   33

Portrait   34

Searching for You   36

Prince Mahasattva on Blood Mountain   37

Dream Book   38

Southern Journal   45

Letter   50

DAMSELFLY, TROUT, HERON

The damselfly folds its wings
over its body when at rest. Captured,
it should not be killed
in cyanide, but allowed to die
slowly: then the colors,
especially the reds and blues,
will last. In the hand
it crushes easily into a rosy
slime. Its powers of flight
are weak. The trout
feeds on the living damselfly.
The trout leaps from the water,
and if there is sun you see
the briefest shiver of gold,
and then the river again.
When the trout dies
it turns its white belly
to the mirror of the sky.
The heron fishes for the trout
in the gravelly shallows on the far
side of the stream. The heron
is the exact blue of the shadows
the sun makes of trees on water.
When you hold the heron most clearly
in your eye, you are least certain
it is there. When the blue heron dies,
it lies beyond reach
on the far side of the river.

BLOOD
MOUNTAIN

A MAY SNOWSTORM

We are awakened this morning by
snow buntings in the lilac bush
and the glassy cold that made us
lie close all winter; and outside
there is brilliance of snow light.
Love, this snow is a short answer:
by now we should know that winter
is always just at the tremulous rim
of the sky ready to spill over
at a mere sneeze, a morning's breath,
as if an inch under the last
white thread of root, or in
the road's nearest hollow, the snow
waits. Blinded by this brightness

we bar the doors, pull curtains,
chain the light out, because we know
that darkness in this disarray of season
becomes us both whose hearts take
awful joy in new grass tufted
with new snow. It ought to remind us
how between one breath and the warm next
the great silence lengthens,
the blood is hindered, and somehow
we do not always resume and awake,
dreaming of snow: that
is what teaches us to love
each other. This dream

in which a mirror, dusted
with new snow, as if struck
and resonating, suddenly
vibrates on the wall,
and the image we are seeing
never wholly subsides. And we
awaken at the last instant
of the last tremor, and outside
something is receding: the freight
from Montreal, a milk truck:
we never know. And in falling

back to sleep we recede
down bright planes of icy glass,
and never by any dawn arrive before
the whole house shivers in the night,
and our faces unfocus into a million
brilliant shards of light. By this
I remind you that with each
breath we are less than ever: now

the days are shrouded in brown spring
sunlight, and I remain shak'n
by wars, the angers not much
diminished: only now
I talk to chairs and pictures,
gesture at stoves and flowerpots from
the vicious asymmetries of breath
and season, my bitterest conviction
and most customary blessing. Love,

I would have lengthened our lives till
the trees spring green again forever,
and the flight of snow geese is high
in the floury blue mornings.
But our bodies walk on their bones
and are busy and clearly
outlive all evidence of breath.
And now the snow flies
after the first warm days. The lie
is bought back, there are between us now
so many awakenings, watery clouds and floods,
turnings of trees, yard soils heaved
by frosts and moles, trout

risen to flies, bodies risen
and laid down again, and snow
laid down as if the resuming breaths
of all of us who sleep in fear of season
freeze in the inclement glass.
May clouds shine in the brown river,
clouds shine, and the paling sun
burns itself out into a ball of gray
crusts that powder at a glance.
And walking now *in diesem wetter*,
in the murderous light of this whole
enkindling sky, I think of you
whose presence has never been
so great a joy as your
departure a darkness. And I
shall be eternally
dejected with it.

A DREAM WITH FURTWÄNGLER IN IT

In this dream the clearing
is somewhere beyond the river Xingu.
It is in the dry part of the forest.
I am standing hidden in a grove
of crecopia and wax palm. Behind me,

just beyond the trees, a nameless
muddy river squirms and coils,
ensnarled in its turns. There are birds
everywhere: sun bittern in the shallows,
bellbirds, scythebills scattering
in the trees. I am looking out

into the clearing: a large white table
stands in its middle, and upon the table
is food broadcast largesse: huge pitchers
of lagers, pilseners, bocks, platters
of sauerbraten, hasenpfeffer, pyramids
of springerles, lebkuchen, piles

of wurst, heaps of spritz. People
are seated at the table, feasting.
I move cautiously from the trees,
preparing myself: there is a great
screeching of green and yellow parrots,
and the people see me, leap up
from the table, stare, smile. I am approached

by a fat man with white mustache
and lederhosen. His mouth is full
of gemengde kloese, crumbs
of vekbroekle pepper his lips.
He raises his stein, he toasts me
in a language I do not fully understand,
I am embraced, led to the table, welcomed

6

by these people. I wish to make them
understand my pleasure, and just
as I begin to speak, I see someone
move in the trees, step into the clearing,
scattering the flock of white arucuana,
and I realize that I have become
someone else, a young and beautiful woman
in the crowd. I see you standing there

just at the edge of the forest, the white
chickens like a cloud around your feet.
Your face is pale as a young moselle. In that instant
I love you. I think you have been lost,
that you may be hungry, and so I heap a plate
with kraut and sulz and gaenseklein,
and fill a mug with beer, and step forward,
and when you stop and hold out your arms,
I think it is for me, and I am faint
with love. I think you see how my hair
is gold as schaum torte mit schlag, my eyes
more brown than anis kuchen. And you

are tall and gaunt and your hair
grows in a white froth of curls
around your ears. You are dressed
entirely in black, and you hold a white baton
in your left hand, and as I drop the food
and move into your arms, you raise them,
bring them down, and behind me the music
begins: *Die Walkure,* the complete
*Die Zauberflote, Das Lied
von der Erde*—I am embarrassed, I do not know

what to do, I had not expected
this. Your eyes are closed, you do not know
that I am here at all, and then, without warning,
the music stops: you have noticed me, dropped
the baton, you move to me, take me in

your arms, bring your face
to mine: you kiss me, and I begin
to fall back, and then, in the middle
of the kiss I look up into your face and you
have become a single cold blue eye—I can see
nothing else: the trees have vanished, the sound
of the river is gone, the clearing is empty,
and it is precisely as if the whole staring open sky
has come down upon me, and I reel back, I am
forced down onto the beery mud of the clearing:
and belly to belly, eye to eye
we writhe on the cold skin of the world.

WEST TOPSHAM

1

In prologue let me plainly say
I shall not ever come to that discretion where
I do not rage to think I grow decrepit,
bursten-bellied, bald and toothless,
thick of hearing, tremulous of leg, dry
and rough-barked as a hemlock slab, the soft rot
setting in and all my wheezy dreams the tunneling
of beetles in a raspy bark. For now
I am fleshed at smaller sports, and grow
in time into the mineral thick fell of earth:
Vermont hairy with violets, roses, lilies and like
minions and darlings of the spring, meantime
working wonders, rousing astonishments. And
being a humble man, I at the same time acknowledge
my miscreate, the nightshades, cabbages and fleaworts
of my plot, though always I try to turn my back and scorn
upon the inkhorn term and speak as is most commonly
received with smile and wink and approbative nod,
not overfine nor at the same time reckless
of the phrase, nor ever ugly, turdy, tut-mouthed,
but always joyous at the goosey brain,
the woolpack of the solid cloud, a crowd, a heap,
a troop, a plume of trees, grass, gulls and rabbits,
in the end, no doubt, a vulgar prattle: but the planet
swells and bulges and protrudes beyond my eyes' aversions,
and tottery, fuddled, always I give up, I am not understood,
or wrongly, out of some general assumption of my innocence.

2

This much I wish to say, my nonsuch nosegay
native sweet, in someway plainer, this is my letter to you,
and out of most severe purpose: the bee,
the honey-stalk, the whole keep of the house
endanger me: the perspectives of the clapboard, the steep
falls of the lawn, the razory apices of ridges,
and the abdominous curves of the meadow into the far
trees. There are ponds below the house, and water runs.
The road crosses the water, and the road
diminishes to the reach of the next farm, and the farm
beyond that, and two miles bearing right or left
somewhere runs Highway 25. I have found my way
with difficulty, I am confused, halfway I have suffered
a failure of vital powers, a swoon, have been
smirked at by the natives, and misdirected. Fitting,
for I always dream of the painless redemption, the return
from fiasco and tumultuous journey to the transcendentally
serene lawns of a transcendentally white house
with columns of oak trees and iron deer and the
affectionate greeting of One who has these many years
waited in full patience without complaint
for me to come in bleeding, dusty and deliquescent
from the fields, the blade in my thigh, or blinded,
the victim of fire or ravenous birds, the lovely blood
on my cheek like tears, one-limbed, a bullet
in my heart, my hands, my head cut off and the dark
pulses of my blood diminishing. Yet never a reproach
for my criminal self-negligence, my careless japeries
and clumsy flounderings: instead, my brow is wiped, my
wounds attended to, blood let, leeches applied: I heal,
I grow strong, I can set forth again renewed, valiant,
sturdy, full of high spirits, lively, gay, spruce

10

in looks, a reveler, a merry prankster, dimpled
in the cheeks from smiling, perfect pilgrim, fit
for the chemistry of Resurrection. Yet
I am of wild and changeful moods. I am perhaps worthy
of being stoned, sometimes. I lie hid and lurk in wait
for the giggling girleries and leap out and shout
and scatter them like chickens from the boot to the safe
and flying four winds. I am easy and fluent
in the telling of lies and let it be said that I roar
and sing scurrilous songs in base places, and shall no doubt
for this little vain merriment find a sorrowful reckoning
in the end. Still, my noises please me, and what
this wretched poet overmuch desires, he easily believes.
It is his conventional cowardice; it makes him
immortally glad. But then he always grows morose
(that is in his favor), he repents, lances his soul, thinks
of the willows and the columned porch and the wind
melliloquent about the chimneys, and you
from where he sits now at the far end
of this small porch of a Federal farmhouse
in this very and summery Vermont.

3

I look down the pitches of the lawn:
fireflies make small explosions in the grass,
and I think that to walk down that slant of lawn
to the black waters of the brook at the dark join
of the cleft would be like dying and that if I die
I will never pardon time. I think my words
will echo only in my own mind forever, to what purpose
I do not know. I see a firefly trapped inside the screen.
I have no name for this. I know it clearly
as I know the dead cry of the starlings

11

in the eaves, the smell of after rain, the warm
air holding in hollows of the roads. For this
there is no name. The holding mind is likewise
without name. That is the final thought,
it is the disorder, the reason
for all this. The clouds
begin to reach up Blood Mountain,
and I am sitting on a farmhouse porch,
and there are trees, and it is late, and I am dreaming.
I dream I stare down into a fouled well and see
the white legbones of a deer and the water's surface
matte with loose hair, the green stink welling
and bellying from the fertile sump up and flowing
outwards in a fountaining current of vines and melons
and leaves and the knotgrass lawns blossoming with gilliflowers,
shoulder-high, cloud-high, the sun finally smothering
in grass, the whole bright field of the sky finally smothering
in grass, and then in the entire silence of this
growth the grasses thickening, darkening, becoming clouds,
reaching up from the ridges. And all night
there is rain. I dream that when I awaken
it is a shining milky day, four roosters
are crowing in your yard and geese
dabble in the green soft muds of the ditches.
This is the literal surface, and for all
the extravagance of what has gone before I now repent,
and make an image: all of Vermont each night
blazes with fireflies, the comet is a faint
green phosphorescence to the North, the catalpas
blossom and each noon the sunlight hardens and the sky
is a clear ground and I can look from my open doorways
into dry and fiery yards. You see, I draw back always,

12

I cannot be understood, *O I wud slepe all the swete darkemans, nor ever speke!* It was as if I had forgotten
to see the steep lawns suddenly erupt in tiny lights,
it was if my fingers burned green and blazed with crushed
fireflies; and as usual no deer appeared. The strict edges
of the meadows held nothing. When I drive home
my carlights sweep the road before me. I override
the long shadows of pebbles and grasses, and the sky
grows long clouds. I drive into the soft explosions
of lightning far to the West at the end of the confusing road
where I will sleep and awaken and sleep. My hands in the
     dashboard
lights are glowing softly green. This whole journey
is before me. I know I am touched with the phosphors
of self-love. The light knows it is light. A great
red moon rides wedged in a crevice of clouds, and I come up
the widening road as if it is the driveway to your house.

FALLING ON BLOOD MOUNTAIN

But you slip in the wet talus
of the lower trail, and bruise
the heel of your palm,
and even if it does not show,
the rock you stopped yourself against
is itself deeply
broken, the shock of your fall
unfolding into the root
of Blood Mountain, and then
deeper; someone on the other
side of the earth awakens
and wonders why and falls
back. Meanwhile, the blood
darkly congeals in the pulsing
root of your hand.

WAITING FOR KOHOUTEK

That night was a clear night
and slowing the car at the top of Depot Hill
and staring to the south, the sky
still lemony over the Adirondacks,
I waited for Kohoutek. Between me

and the mountain Miles' fields
were frozen into a riffled ice. There
was nothing in the sky.
Holding my arm out, looking
for a patchy brightness small

enough to cover with my fingertip,
I found nothing, though Venus
elegantly burned over the southern ridges,
and the wind burst on the windows,
and I stayed in the shuddering car

watching for the comet only
a little longer. Whatever
the promises had been, nothing
ever came of them. Orion
flickered in the lower sky

and next morning I found
in the freezing center of the road
a Holstein bull calf, newly born,
lying with his legs neatly tucked
like something from a crèche,

shiny as china, at that angle
of the cold sun, from that
distance, but close up matted
with barn dirt and shivering, three
starry drops of blood strung in a row

on a foreleg. He must have fallen
from Miles' pickup. Some mornings
near dawn the old man drives
a load of calves for slaughtering,
and lost this one from the truck,

not noticing because he drove East,
blind into the sun, and the sun
at the top of Depot Hill rises
mornings as I always imagined
the comet would rise, in horns

of light and at the enormous arc
of the rising center the tangled
curls of its incandescent poll. Now,
watching for the comet over Miles' icy fields,
eyes frozen bright as china, I can feel

the fat blood dwindle. Nothing happens,
only out there in the cold fall
of its farthest swing, smaller than
a fingertip, a lion's roar of light,
maned and billowing beyond all brightness flies

out again beyond the farthest I
will ever see. In all the space around Polaris
swing the Bull, the Lion, and the Hunter hangs
steady in the lower sky. On these
cold nights I stay inside, containing

my own spaces, and the wind
that pours down Depot Hill from Miles' fields
bears and rings on the loose lights
of my windows, as the comet might with fire
have rung my eyes.

16

VERTIGO ON BLOOD MOUNTAIN

At the top of Blood Mountain I stare into
the flight of invisible ranges to the East,
into the red sun. I can't live
in a place like this for long. It is
too high, and I always feel that I am
falling off, that if I don't lie down
. and belly into the stone, my fingers
in crevices, my cheek crushing saxifrage
and lupines, I will sail slowly down
spread out flat like a great kite,
sideslip to a crash landing in
the pines below. I'll be dead,
I'll be dead, and if I would mourn
for you, think how for myself and what
galas of dismal ceremony for
my poor pierced belly and
attendant bones.

EARLY MORNING POEM

Mightily detained and allured,
I have listened to music all night,
Bix and Tram to expel austerity,
Bechet to inform the manner,
Wild Bill Davison, then Messiaen,
Haydn for grace and comeliness,
a little Chopin for
the continuity, two hours
of Bruckner, and Schumann
for the last of the wine. By two,

everything thinning and thickening,
ragged space at the edges
of things, the sofa billowing four
inches off the floor, the air
a little milky, I stand
at the door staring across
the lawns at whole distance,
the raucous, bristling landscapes
to the north, boulders, maple
forests, streams flooding
in between. I imagine
I move out, accompanied,

the circling Bear apace,
the Hunter flourishing
his bow. Dogs bark
around me all night long,
and then at dawn the sun

squirms from a black
seed onto the highest comb
of the farthest peak, and all
this time I have been coming

closer, wondering how to announce
myself, afraid I will choke
on a clot of voice, close
my eyes, pitch forward. But by noon
I shall nearly have arrived,
and at the last instant, my hand
on your door, I will find myself
precisely back where I was
at this near center: sofa, table,
a lamp, the fireplace. It is late
beyond late, the poem after five days
still does not work, the cat is scratching
to get in, there are mice
in the cornflakes. Tonight
music has been something
of an answer: the dense
speechless collisions, the mind
delicately bellowing on its fixed
centers. I think it is

by no means certain that the centers
change, being only discovered
and rediscovered—we are afraid,
at one of them, of ice, of silence,

of rivers at night,
of drowning; at another I know
there is nothing final about grief
any more than about longing. I ask
at this center what there is
to see? I try not
to see. Instead I turn back
to the room, and hear strings
everywhere, horns
sonorous in the corners,
the tympani like something bearing
on the doors. And there is no voice
to trouble us.

BAD WEATHER ON BLOOD MOUNTAIN

It is cold on the top of Blood Mountain, almost
the verge of snow, and you are bored because
your friends have gone down before you
and your fire is almost out, and so you try
imagining that you are not on Blood Mountain,
but on Everest, the Climber torn from his holds
and swept by the terrible snow plumes of the Summit.
You imagine your mask carried away and your eyes
frozen instantly into a million perfectly hexagonal
lenses of ice and you stare at your million hands
and one by one the fingers crack in little bloody
hairlines at the knuckles, and break away. You find it
strange that there are no visions. You feel yourself
being slowly buried by the wind, the snow is up
to your thighs, your breasts, and soon you are breathing
snow and asking yourself when you will grow angry, hungry,
frightened, want love? You realize that after this
for all time whenever you lie down, Mount Everest
will heave beneath you, roaring with ice and stone,
its snows exploding from the raw peak. And then, thank God,
you notice that here on Blood Mountain the weather
improves a little, the rocky sky softens and begins
to drift to the east, showing gold and yellow where
the clouds crack and break away. The wind is turning,
Blood Brook is beginning to clear. It is a great relief,
and you are happy because you know that in a few hours
you can see again over a northern forest of beech and maple,
leaves mostly shed, the colors of rock and lichen. You tell yourself

this is a hard climate, but not relentless. You hesitate
on the steep hard spine of the trail, wanting to go neither up
nor down, and then the rain stops entirely, and directly
before you, thrust up through a sudden towering of white clouds,
the sun appears, and it is trailing a great wind plume of
gold and yellow fires, and still you cannot decide.

THE FIRE

That night you dream of smoke,
and by almost dawn—awakening,
your eyes still closed—you're furious,
feel like revenge, like screaming
at someone who knows you are fully ready
to kill him, and who shrinks from your rage
into the dream.

And suddenly you are awake,
and the room is layered with smoke
and you cannot breathe, and you know
the rage in your dream was terror, and you rise
shouting at everyone to go,
get out, your wife hauling at doors,
the kids, the dog frantic on the stairs.

But they run out into the calm yards,
and you are left alone, there
in the unnatural heat of the stairwell.
You close your eyes, and unerringly blind,
make your way down into the cellar hole
under the house. And you find,
when you open your eyes again, it is like
facing the one thing still alive
besides yourself, to see the fire
heaving behind the sills. And at
the precise moment that you confront it
it explodes upward into the space between
the walls. You realize then that this fire
has been waiting for you for a long time,
through years of your sleeping
and waking and sleeping again.

Now you choke in the deepening
smoke, and here in the swampy cellar room
you face the fire at last, appalled,
and it joyously capers and dances and flies
into the tender darknesses between your walls.
And you are afraid to come closer. You think:
"It is all going to burn now!" and *"Why not?"*
After all, it has always been like this,
the dull nucleus of fire locked
into the basement beams of whatever house
you have lived in, working its slow way out.

But this is the first time you have surely met.
You stand with a too-short garden hose,
ankle-deep in cellar mud, and wet
the timbers down. The fire dies,
it faces you and flares, subsides,
reaches for the floor joists
and the hemlock lath. The lightbulb dims,
the useless water splatters on hot stone
and steams, the fire blossoms, and you shout
into the darkness and the crazy flames:
"Go out go out go out go out!"

TOUTES LES LUMIÈRES

The trees touch overhead
and stars are locked
in the angles of branches. City

lights are in the far
distance. Overhead,
a lamp snows light

onto the street. There is
a moon. You stand
in the white circle

of its light. You wear
a white lace gown,
and you are gesturing toward me.

Your shadow falls
behind you, away from me,
and to your right, a red house

bulks, all its windows
lighted. Plants grow
in the windows, and the light

is torn by leaves that are
like knives. The edge
of the circle in which

you stand is set
with burning oil lamps.
There are blue shadows

between your fingers, at
your throat, but your face
is pale as the moon

and you are smiling
at me. But I stand
in the shadows at this end

of the street, and do not
move, because behind you,
at the far end, I can see

a woman with her back turned,
her shadow toward me. She
is standing in a circle

of white light, she wears
a white gown, and she is
holding out her hand to

someone I cannot see.

AT THE TOP OF BLOOD MOUNTAIN

In December when I come on its coldest
first day to the leafless peak of Blood Mountain
and find it furry with clouds, what
will I do? Will I smell on my fingers
the smoke of the fire I built this morning
with red maple chunks and cedar splits?
I will watch the water of Blood Brook begin
and break on the pebbles and descend.
I will feel the black mold at the trail's edge
and find it warm almost to fire with the slow rot
of dropped leaves. I will think
that beasts hide in the stones,
and it will be hard for me to breathe,
resting there at the end of the path,
staring out into the raw and smoky mists
between me and the next peak. I will suspect
I might feel better if I drank from Blood Brook,
if I slept for a time in the warm
trailside soil. Instead, I find myself
a hemlock to lean against, breathless. I hear
the faint cries of the climbers who will never
arrive. Then, as the day hardens
and the sun begins to organize the sky, red yet
as a maple fire and burning
with the same slow difficulty, I will
give way to my illness: I will feel cold
from the wood I thought burning, and begin
to think how from this hemlock where I stand,
at the always and unbalancing center of
this rooted hemlock, I am in some regard of time
forced to the descent of my difficult breath.
Staring straight up the trunk into the perfect
spiral climb of the branches to their

terrible conclusion high over the mountain
and my head, I think crazily of descent,
of a whelk's shell, God's-eye, spin of maple seed
and the hemlock's green leaf-needles "that will
outlast the winter." I will stand unbalancing
into the right of time at the eyed
and rooted center of Blood Mountain
in the precise middle of all this green
and stony, winged, embracing, clawed
and calling out of which surrounds me, and fall
into the one fixed center of heretofore not
present always and beloved you.

THE INTRUDER

Each time I come by chance
into the place where someone lives,
I find the bedclothes disarranged,
the mark of her head fresh in the warm pillow,
the smell of cooking just beginning to fade.
I never doubt she will return at any minute,
surprised to find the door still open,
pile her groceries on the kitchen table,
pull off her gloves, walk through the rooms
unhurried, clearly confident that she is being
foolish, that no one is truly hiding
in the place where she lives. She is not
intent: I hear her empty an ashtray, snap
a light switch, brush at a curtain. And each time
this is the moment I would like to step out
into the room where she is, and smile at her,
knowing she will think it no more
than a stupid error of inattention
that brings me here. Each time
I imagine she smiles back at me,
takes my arm, escorts me to the couch,
offers me tea and cookies. But I cannot
reassure myself that this is the way
it happens. My particular fear
is that before I can smile or say a word
she will scream, grow pale, fall back from me,
her hands before her face, scramble
undignifiedly about the room for something
to kill me with, her face ugly with rage;
or turn on me coldly and demand
an explanation, tell me I have no right
to be here. This last
is the greater fear: what do I know

that I can say plainly? Why
am I here? I know that I have come into this place
from a place I cannot remember, where I must
have risen from my bed, washed, put on
my clothes, eaten my breakfast, walked out
into the street, glanced at myself
in shop windows, avoided children
and dogs, thought about flowers, the weather,
walked purposefully without stumbling on curbstones,
and arrived. I can remember none of this.
I do not know if it has happened
in just this way. I hear her moving toward
the room where I am standing. In a moment
she will turn the knob, open the door, see me.
I will be neither hiding nor waiting.
I will smile at her. Perhaps
I will tell her that I bear a name
as well as this unexpected presence.
I will tell her
that this time I cannot leave.

PHOTOGRAPH WHEN YOU
ARE NOT LOOKING

As if in a photograph—taken
when you are not aware, by one
who contrives to stay

out of your sight, peering at you
from thickets of tall grass, leaping
from behind trees to focus, snap

the shutter, vanish into the shadows
of hydrangea—you are caught
with your face beautifully inclined,

your hands busy with food, a flower,
anything at all, your hair
untidy. If you knew you would turn

and say to the bare street,
the bare fields, speaking firmly
in a clear voice, knowing

you will be heard: *"I do not wish
to be seen!"* And as you speak
you will notice that from the depths

of a rose trellis, from behind
the lattice of an old porch is coming
a soft *click* and *click* and *click,*

in one latent image your hand
rising, your mouth just beginning
to open, in another your eyes

staring directly into the lens,
which is in that instant bright
as a rose with the sun, as blinding.

31

And there is nothing you can do
but turn and walk away and even then
this is what the last photograph
will show: the street empty before you
and the light gone bad.

DAWN ON BLOOD MOUNTAIN

Owls dived at my eyes.
I still breathe the air
their wings moved.
At dawn on the bare
mountain the day is not
beautiful. Clouds in thin
ribbons blacken half
the sky. A yellow skin
of sunlight covers
half the trail. I have not seen
a sky like this before.
I don't know what I mean
to say *you are beautiful.*
I am blind.
I know you by touching
your face. You are blind.
My fingers cover
where your eyes might be.
Your hair is bright
to my hand. Try not to see.
What is there to see?
I turn to go
down. I am
a contriver.
You know.

PORTRAIT

Let me describe you
to yourself: let me
tell you how you are
seen: let me begin

with your hands, they are
small and pale and smooth
and I imagine them filled
with a light soil, a yellow
sandy loam, the grains

sifting between your fingers.
Your hair is more difficult:
I think of it as I might imagine
apple leaves brushing
my face. Your arms

gather timothy in August:
you hold the sweet grass to you
with your arms. Your feet
are for walking on mosses,
leaf molds, beds of partridge berry,
your legs for being brushed
by wild chicory and daisies,
and with your tongue you may
have tasted jewelweed. Now

I become guarded—I think
of the wind shattering itself
on pines, the folding of hills,
everywhere the relentless
currentings, risings of water,
coursing of small streams
through the tunnels of alder
and cedar. I imagine

your shoulders in my hands:
I have held the warm porcelains
of moon cowrie from the Eniwetok
reefs. I imagine your breasts,

your belly, and I think
how the full rain washes dust
from an October day, I am forced
to a consideration of meadows,
a swirling of pools, the clear
nakedness of snowfields. I cannot

satisfy my single purpose here:
I go to your eyes, shadow upon
shadow upon shadow, in your eyes
a road in moonlight plunging steeply
between pines. Your face

is an open shade. I see
patches of white sunlight on the floors
of hemlock woods. Your smile
is motionless at the center
of your smile, your ears
are covered by your hair:

you hear the sounds of twigs,
seedpods, apples falling. My hand
is on your cheek, your throat,
the warm hollow of your back. Now
I am at the beginning, you summon

a life so deep within me
I have come to believe the least
sequence of flesh occurs
as my most fragile artifice. Therefore

I move to touch you, and I find
your body light upon its bones.

35

SEARCHING FOR YOU

In early spring, the mountain is
flooded. Water sheets on the rocks,
and the higher meadows become lakes,
and it is no use to search for anything.
But in summer I watch in the sandy
light woods near the edge
of the forest. Later, I look
along the forest roads; in the warm
days of autumn, I begin to watch closely
the scrubby slopes, the exposed soil
among mosses. Then, toward winter,
I search among the trunks of pines,
firs and spruces, sometimes in oak woods,
sometimes in the groves of sweet chestnuts
or under larches, never where maple
and hornbeam grow. Not rarely,
in the high grasses that grow
in limestone soils, I think
I have found signs.
But I have always
been mistaken.

PRINCE MAHASATTVA
ON BLOOD MOUNTAIN

Where the pine forest grows to
the very edge of the precipice on Blood
Mountain I see Prince Mahasattva remove
his crimson robe and hang it on the branch
of a tree not yet come into leaf. I do not
know what kind of a tree it is. I see him
leap from the precipice: his sash
trails behind him like a delicate
twisted flame. Below, in the valley,
a starving tigress with her seven cubs
is waiting. About the head and body
of Prince Mahasattva are flowers like birds or
birds like flowers. The tigress
is watching the body of Prince Mahasattva
in flight: his body arches
like a bent bow, his eyes close,
and he reaches out with his hands
for the waiting beast, or he is
praying, or both.

DREAM BOOK

The first dream
is always of God: it is
said to be a sure sign
of death. You may never
frustrate this design.
The second
is of blood flowering
in the corner of your right
eye: *it means:* mediocrity
in love and fortune. There
are other and lesser dreams.
They all imply your dissolution.

The dream of being blind
has no significance, and should
on every occasion be ignored.
It is the only dream
of its kind. Never allow it
to confuse or afflict you.

To dream on the same night
of butchers, of bright buttons,
of letting birds out of a cage
is a dream warning. *It warns*
that a step imprudently taken
may embitter the remainder
of your life.

To dream of bones
is of such clear and ordinary
significance,
we will waste no time upon it here.

For a married woman to dream
her arms have grown lusty
denotes: that she will have
many sons, few of whom
will survive her. If she dreams
she is driving a chariot
drawn by falcons, salmon, and pigs
it means: that her husband will arrive
at public honors, will grow rich,
will make friends, will love
this woman.

To dream of fish is rather
unfavorable, especially
to lovers, since it is
indicative of death
to the sick, and loss of love
to the young. It is forewarning
of that of which
at present
you know nothing.

To dream of the dead
is a certain sign
that you will be
unable to give warning
of danger, except
to your enemies.

To dream of rivers
of red mud is the same
as dreaming of the dead.

It is not understood
what it means to dream
of yellow flowers.

39

But should you at one
and the same time dream
of all these things:
redbirds freed and flashing
like gold buttons, butchers
stone-blind and lying
in the strong arms of married
women, dead boys floating
face down in the red streams
nibbled by fishes, rivers rising
over their jonquil banks, the trees
drowning, growing silvery
as forests of bone: *then:*
prepare yourself for some
great and important change in your
condition, prospects and circumstances.
Whether it be for the better
or worse, time alone
can tell. But the change
will be as great and sudden
as it is unexpected.

In the dream
she opens these doors:
she sees that the cage
is made of thin bamboo slivers.
She feels what it must be like
for one of these yellow slivers
to tear open her eyes: the sky
a red explosion, and then
darkness like a flurry
of wings. Now the light
tears at her face like beaks,
and the sun shrinks.

40

into millions of points, intense
as the eyes of falcons. The sky
is nothing but wings. The sky
is a thickening flurry of wings,
and the sun blossoms,
gold, at the interstices.

If I am the butcher: I lie down
in my own blood. My spine
burns in my back like a great
cleaver dividing me. I love
this woman, though
I do not know her name.
I move in her slick flesh
slowly, till I die. Or she
dies. Sometimes
I dream. My dreams
are red. Everything is red.
Except my hands are white
as tallow. In the end
my own gross meat gives way
to the infinite cleanliness
of bone. Be ready for the next
dream. It is not hers.
She never sleeps.

It is my dream: he stinks
of stale chops, of black
pudding. I think
of other things: I think
of rivers and the fish
in these rivers and the scoured
stone of these rivers. There
is something else, but I
cannot remember it. He

41

is heavy on me as if I
were the lakebed of the planet
and he the whole weight
of its waters. *If I
had sons:* if I had sons
they would be dead, like me.
If they did not die at once
I would myself kill them.
His eyes are white, like lard.
Hairs sprout from his grease.

O in the lovely midst of our most
innocent delightful play, all time
forgotten, our tasty dinners waiting,
we felt the air grow thick, the shadow
of the floods overwhelm us, and now
we are dead. Who
will do us a courtesy? (Because
this is only a dream, I
will speak for them: it is easy
I know to pretend drowning.
I will have them remember first
that the feathery sky is always
at their backs, and they
will be staring down into the clear
yellow gravels of the riverbed.
A stonefly will climb on an ear,
an early brown caddis will hide
in the dry hair patch on the back
of a head. Now I will make it
that the corners of their eyes
bulge with blood, that they have given
up breathing, and see more clearly than
I see. They see among other things

the salmon swelling with her eggs,
and the otter gorge himself
on salmon. And I give
something of myself to this. I
take on voices: *"We
are the children of this woman
who gives herself to blood,
and our breath
was always sharp
as fishbones in our
throats. Now
we are dead."*)

I sweep at the gravels
with the great caudal. If I
on the redd and the cock fish
beside me should dream
we are stared down upon by the eyes
of drowned children: *then this dream means:*
our river will become blood,
and the spawning gravels compact
into rock, and the rock grow sharp
as an otter's teeth, and night become
the darkness of his jaws. We
are hungry. We feed. And the water
we breathe is sweet with the breath
they have given up to it. This
is true, and not a dream.

I am the dreamer of all this,
and cannot even dream the truth.
I want to say: I should never
have laid hands on any of you.
I should have killed you first.

43

I should have drowned you in stone.
I should have made you grow fins,
face into currents, split
along the clear axis of your white
spines. This is a dream. This
is a dream: *it means:* night
has come down once and for all
and the windows bulge inward
from the pressure of darkness,
and to fly in the face of this dream
is, to say it plainly, death,
or it is love, or blindness, or
I feel the weight of my own body
or my own body. I wash
downstream. The dream
means no more than this.
I have given up breathing.
My belly is scaled.
My arms feather, and I fly
in the red water higher
and higher. This
is a dream. *It means:*
it could not possibly
be true. I will die
blind.

SOUTHERN JOURNAL

1

The first thing I notice:
everything whistles with birds.
The first morning
I am looking in my mirror,
and a quail calls
outside the window. I run
to the window, but he
is gone. It is the first
time in my life. During
this one day
I do not know
the names of trees.

2

Juncos come to the feeder
and a tanager blurs
like a hummingbird at the suet.
The second night I have a dream:
I wake up shouting at a dun-colored fox
which runs away, looking over
a winged shoulder at me.
Apart from this
in the dream are no birds.
Everywhere I sense water.

3

The third night I am traveling.
It is raining. Trees
shatter into leaf. I see
myself in the watery planes
of the window glass,

and ahead on the highway
a red light flickers on and off
like a cardinal at the dark
heart of a pine.

4
Whenever I taste rain, I look
for my face: in puddles,
hallway mirrors, the bowls
of spoons. The planet
is shining with water,
and I have a dream
that in one grove the pines
become a forest of herons,
beaks straight up, their feet
fast in the earth. The needles
bloom into feathers,
and the trees shudder and flap
and take flight, trailing
long white roots like herons' legs.
They rise and cry out far
above me, flocking south.
I am left to choke
in a rust-colored dust,
and nothing is left to make shadows.
This is on the fourth day.

5
The next morning when the sun comes out
I cross two rivers in pink spate.
I see jonquils blooming white
from an orange soil. I think
snow may be falling
in Vermont. Wherever

I am is a difficult
climate, perhaps
relentless, and breathing
is hard. I try
to tell you that what I mean
by "the nature of yearning" is
"the horror of longing," or
"blindness." Until now
I have lied about this.

6

The third dream is that
I want to grow wings and a curved
yellow beak, cast a monstrous
shadow, darken
entire mountains, watch houses
empty and people point
up at me, crying out. My
feathers will shine in the sun,
green as new leaves, and at
my first sight of the sea,
I will flare up, screaming. I dream
it is the last and hunting pattern
I possess.

7

At this point the heart
somewhat diminishes, grows
more regular, falls back into
orderly plasms of recollection:
I am walking alone
for quail, in Indiana, sighting
along the corn rows for the feeding
coveys. The November corn rustles

like feathers, and the sun
is brown over the cold fields.
Sometimes snow is falling,
sometimes the wind is like snow.
I have always lived in places like this,
where, despite the cold, the ice
on the fields, the birds are there,
black vigorous specks far
at the ends of the rows,
and I run to flush them,
battering at the dried stalks,
startled at the flare.
It takes time for me to breathe again.
In such a manner
I am using up time
at an incredible rate.
It is how I measure longing.

8

South of you: in one
bus station I see a fat
red-headed porter who is blind,
who never had eyes. His head
is like a huge pale kidney,
and he stands over the fountain,
his thumb on the button,
listening to the curve
of the water. He is clearly
amazed. He whistles
a bobwhite call over and over,
and then he kisses the water.
He never drinks. I am reading
my book, and I hear a quail

calling, and I look up
and he is there, being astonished,
brushing the water with his lips,
whistling to it like a bird.

9

Whatever I do I leave
you, wherever I am the rivers
swell and the trees drop leaves
like feathers of a sort
I have not seen before. I do not
expect to breathe only for myself.
I am easily astonished, this
is a new land, that
tangles me. We
are eating and drinking together,
and I look into the dry
convergences of this place
and where on my lawns the snow
grows like a flowering of salt,
the quail come to whistle
like water like water like water!

LETTER

My dear friend: notwithstanding
long silence, my thoughts
have been with you. Doubtless
all has been well with you,
or I would have known. As for me,
there is little to tell. I have
nothing but praise for the weather:
much sun, a little rain, and the garden
a full and green exuberance.
I have been able to see Blood Mountain
for over a week. The streams
are low and run clear,
and the first hatch of yellow mayfly
is due from the riffles tomorrow.
Last night a luna moth came to the lantern,
and at noon two hummingbirds
perched for an instant in the wild apple.
I suppose what I mean is that everywhere
I look, something is moving, a fact
which occupies my mind, not precisely
the oil and wine of consolation. If I

for example play Schumann's Third Symphony
through the open window, its molecules
instantly disperse, the horns thinning
in the hayfield, the trumpets dying
in the pines. Motion is always away from:
and beyond the pines, high up on the side
of the mountain, nothing can be heard.
But inside, the house is engorged
with music; the music cannot fully
escape and beats back on itself, wall
to wall, the doors shuddering
with sound, the windows trembling. This

50

music overspreads the ceilings like shadows,
and glances like sunlight from the tabletops.
This is how things move in the dark
house of the skull, all the pines and birds
and mornings of the world straining
at masonries, overflowing cornices, only
a little, finally, leaking to the hillsides,
the rest moving toward the darkness that is
everywhere, the quiet, the melancholy
annihilations. Now

the thought arises that this time of silence
has been as narrow a movement
as the silence itself, and knowing this
has made it hard for me to speak:
but have you never felt that you breathe
your air through water? I suffer
that necessity. Do you often think
how many of the erstwhile breathing have
this very instant suffocated
and fallen in their graves? I know
you understand the frequent
real helplessness: the grave
is nothing, only the discovered
weakness, and you and I have known it
all along. You see
how I argue myself into an awkward
situation? It is because I am lost
to the sweet testimony.
Things move: I close

my eyes for an instant and shadows
leap on the walls. I feel
a weight of cloud race in

from the west, from across the lake,
and the wind rises, sharply. The willows
hiss in the far corner of the yard. I sit
with the memory of light behind
my eyes, the recollection
of fair weather. There is
a difference of climes, and it
is growing late, and before long
night will have fallen like an austere
and bitter accident. But I do not wish to close
before I tell you how the shadows
of the high clouds are like
dark lake beds, on the eastern ridges
of the mountain. Here,

where I live, where the river
on its last run to the lake cuts through
the stone ledges of the ancient beach,
the skeletons of whales have been found. Let me
tell you a dream: I am walking
through the thin sea of the hayfield,
and then I climb, and near the top
of the mountain, in the dark mud
of a drying lake, I see without
astonishment a slow surging
of flukes, and then the gleam
of a vast white belly, and the sun
breaks through, and before me
in an open meadow the last spout of the whale
rises like a great stone tree. Tomorrow's
dream will be of you climbing to see
what swims in the shadows of the high clouds;
and you will find only the mark
of water. My dreams

overspread the walls, and it
is growing late. There are fireflies
in the grass. In the thin blue vase
on the table, the second bud of the white iris
has begun to open. The morning's blossom
crumples softly on itself,
and what I can see: the white flower,
the brown wood of the ceiling darkening
around the nails, night flooding in
upon Blood Mountain—I let
enter me for contrivance. In the end
this place is as strangely good
as I am, in practice, strangely
not. I seem to bring night on myself
as some kind of desperate maneuver,
causing the moon to rise, and the Pleiades,
allowing darkness to overspread the lawns
and fill the stream beds. Well,
my arrangements sustain no one
but myself. I walk out into the yard

and stand beside the well. At the bottom
the water shines like oil. The water
swallows pebbles and dirt clumps,
the sunlight in the yard pours down
into the well, and the water
swallows it. Soon
the yard will be dark. If I
put my ear to the grass and listen
for water running the deep channels,
the grass will roar in my ear,
and there will be the sound
of something with jaws
feeding an inch below the white

fabric of the roots. I will be able to hear
nothing else. The music is caught
in the trees high up on the side
of the mountain, and the slow
bubbles of my breath rise
to the surface of the atmosphere
and burst, silently. This is why
I must close. Assuredly, it is not
to turn from you, but
a thing I offer, as I tell you how
the sun is low and the first breeze
of a hot day moves down from the pines,
warm with the smell of resin. We will,
no doubt, not hear from one another.

PITT POETRY SERIES

Dannie Abse, *Collected Poems*   Cloth, ISBN 0-8229-3333-2, $9.95/Paper, ISBN 0-8229-5276-2, $3.95

Adonis, *The Blood of Adonis*   Cloth, ISBN 0-8229-3213-X, $6.95/Paper, ISBN 0-8229-5220-3, $2.95

Jack Anderson, *The Invention of New Jersey*   Cloth, ISBN 0-8229-3168-0, $6.95/Paper, ISBN 0-8229-5203-3, $2.95

Jon Anderson, *Death & Friends*   Cloth, ISBN 0-8229-3202-4, $6.95/Paper, ISBN 0-8229-5217-3, $2.95

Jon Anderson, *In Sepia*   Cloth, ISBN 0-8229-3278-4, $6.95/Paper, ISBN 0-8229-5245-9, $2.95

Jon Anderson, *Looking for Jonathan*   Cloth, ISBN 0-8229-3141-9, $6.95/Paper, ISBN 0-8229-5139-8, $2.95

John Balaban, *After Our War*   Paper, ISBN 0-8229-5247-5, $2.95

Gerald W. Barrax, *Another Kind of Rain*   Cloth, ISBN 0-8229-3206-7, $6.95/Paper, ISBN 0-8229-5218-1, $2.95

Leo Connellan, *First Selected Poems*   Paper, ISBN 0-8229-5268-8, $2.95

Michael Culross, *The Lost Heroes*   Paper, ISBN 0-8229-5251-3, $2.95

Fazıl Hüsnü Dağlarca, *Selected Poems*   Paper, ISBN 0-8229-5204-1, $2.95

James Den Boer, *Learning the Way*   Cloth, ISBN 0-8229-3140-0, $6.95/Paper, 0-8229-5138-X, $2.95

James Den Boer, *Trying to Come Apart*   Cloth, ISBN 0-8229-3216-4, $6.95/Paper, ISBN 0-8229-5221-1, $2.95

Norman Dubie, *Alehouse Sonnets*   Cloth, ISBN 0-8229-3226-1, $6.95/Paper, ISBN 0-8229-5223-8, $2.95

Norman Dubie, *In the Dead of the Night*   Paper, ISBN 0-8229-5261-0, $2.95

Odysseus Elytis, *The Axion Esti*   Cloth, ISBN 0-8229-3283-0, $7.50/Paper, ISBN 0-8229-5252-1, $3.50

John Engels, *Blood Mountain*   Cloth, ISBN 0-8229-3338-1, $6.95/Paper, ISBN 0-8229-5277-7, $2.95/Special Binding, ISBN 0-8229-3289-X, $30.00

John Engels, *The Homer Mitchell Place*   Cloth, ISBN 0-8229-3149-4, $6.95/Paper, ISBN 0-8229-5159-2, $2.95

John Engels, *Signals from the Safety Coffin*   Cloth, ISBN 0-8229-3291-1, $6.95/Paper, ISBN 0-8229-5255-6, $2.95

Abbie Huston Evans, *Collected Poems*   ISBN 0-8229-3208-3, $7.95

Brendan Galvin, *No Time for Good Reasons*   Paper, ISBN 0-8229-5250-5, $2.95

Gary Gildner, *Digging for Indians*   Cloth, ISBN 0-8229-3230-X, $6.95/Paper, ISBN 0-8229-5224-6, $2.95

Gary Gildner, *First Practice*   Cloth, ISBN 0-8229-3179-6, $6.95/Paper, ISBN 0-8229-5208-4, $2.95

Gary Gildner, *Nails*   Cloth, ISBN 0-8229-3293-8, $6.95/Paper, ISBN 0-8229-5257-2, $2.95

Mark Halperin, *Backroads*   Cloth, ISBN 0-8229-3311-X, $6.95/Paper, ISBN 0-8229-5266-1, $2.95

Michael S. Harper, *Dear John, Dear Coltrane*   Paper, ISBN, 0-8229-5213-0, $2.95

Michael S. Harper, *Song: I Want a Witness*   Cloth, ISBN 0-8229-3254-7, $6.95/Paper, ISBN 0-8229-5231-9, $2.95

Samuel Hazo, *Blood Rights*   Cloth, ISBN 0-8229-3147-8, $6.95/Paper, ISBN 0-8229-5157-6, $2.95

Samuel Hazo, *Once for the Last Bandit: New and Previous Poems*   ISBN 0-8229-3240-7, $6.95

Samuel Hazo, *Quartered*   Cloth, ISBN 0-8229-3284-9, $6.95/Paper, ISBN 0-8229-5253-X, $2.95

Gwen Head, *Special Effects*   Paper, ISBN 0-8229-5258-0, $2.95

Milne Holton and Graham W. Reid, eds., *Reading the Ashes: An Anthology of the Poetry of Modern Macedonia*   Cloth, ISBN 0-8229-3337-3, $8.95/ Paper, ISBN 0-8229-5282-3, $3.50

Shirley Kaufman, *The Floor Keeps Turning*   ISBN 0-8229-3190-7, $6.95

Shirley Kaufman, *Gold Country*   Cloth, ISBN 0-8229-3269-5, $6.95/Paper, ISBN 0-8229-5238-6, $2.95

Abba Kovner, *A Canopy in the Desert: Selected Poems*   Cloth, ISBN 0-8229-3260-1, $8.95/Paper, ISBN 0-8229-5232-7, $3.95

Paul-Marie Lapointe, *The Terror of the Snows: Selected Poems*   Cloth, ISBN 0-8229-3327-6, $7.95/Paper, ISBN 0-8229-5274-2, $2.95

Larry Levis, *Wrecking Crew*   Cloth, ISBN 0-8229-3238-5, $6.95/Paper, ISBN 0-8229-5226-2, $2.95

Jim Lindsey, *In Lieu of Mecca*   Paper, ISBN 0-8229-5267-X, $2.95

Tom Lowenstein, tr., *Eskimo Poems from Canada and Greenland*   ISBN 0-8229-1110-8, $6.95

Archibald MacLeish, *The Great American Fourth of July Parade*   Paper, ISBN 0-8229-5272-6, $3.95/Record, $5.95

Judith Minty, *Lake Songs and Other Fears*   Paper, ISBN 0-8229-5242-4, $2.95

James Moore, *The New Body*   Paper, ISBN 0-8229-5260-2, $2.95

Carol Muske, *Camouflage*   Paper, ISBN 0-8229-5259-9, $2.95

Thomas Rabbitt, *Exile*   Cloth, ISBN 0-8229-3292-X, $6.95/Paper, ISBN 0-8229-5256-4, $2.95

Belle Randall, *101 Different Ways of Playing Solitaire and Other Poems*   Cloth, ISBN 0-8229-3261-X, $6.95/Paper, ISBN 0-8229-5235-1, $2.95

Ed Roberson, *Etai-Eken*   Paper, ISBN 0-8229-5263-9, $2.95

Ed Roberson, *When Thy King Is A Boy*   Cloth, ISBN 0-8229-3197-4, $6.95/Paper, ISBN 0-8229-5214-9, $2.95

Eugene Ruggles, *The Lifeguard in the Snow*   Cloth, ISBN 0-8229-3336-5, $6.95/Paper, ISBN 0-8229-5281-5, $2.95/Special Binding, ISBN 0-8229-3340-3, $30.00

Dennis Scott, *Uncle Time*   Cloth, ISBN 0-8229-3271-7, $6.95/Paper, ISBN 0-8229-5240-8, $2.95

Herbert Scott, *Disguises*   Paper, ISBN 0-8229-5248-3, $2.95
Herbert Scott, *Groceries*   Cloth, ISBN 0-8229-3332-2, $6.95/Paper, ISBN
0-8229-5270-X, $2.95
Richard Shelton, *Of All the Dirty Words*   Cloth, ISBN 0-8229-3248-2,
$6.95/Paper, ISBN 0-8229-5230-0, $2.95
Richard Shelton, *The Tattooed Desert*   Cloth, ISBN 0-8229-3212-1, $6.95/
Paper, ISBN 0-8229-5219-X, $2.95
Richard Shelton, *You Can't Have Everything*   Cloth, ISBN 0-8229-3309-8,
$6.95/Paper, ISBN 0-8229-5262-9, $2.95
Gary Soto, *The Elements of San Joaquin*   Cloth, ISBN 0-8229-3335-7,
$6.95/Paper, ISBN 0-8229-5279-3, $2.95/Special Binding, ISBN 0-8229-
3339-X, $30.00
David Steingass, *American Handbook*   Cloth, ISBN 0-8229-3270-9, $6.95/
Paper, ISBN 0-8229-5239-4, $2.95
David Steingass, *Body Compass*   Cloth, ISBN 0-8229-3180-X, $6.95/Paper,
ISBN 0-8229-5209-2, $2.95
Tomas Tranströmer, *Windows & Stones: Selected Poems*   Cloth, ISBN
0-8229-3241-5, $6.95/Paper, ISBN 0-8229-5228-9, $2.95
Alberta T. Turner, *Learning to Count*   Paper, ISBN 0-8229-5249-1, $2.95
Marc Weber, *48 Small Poems*   Cloth, ISBN 0-8229-3257-1, $6.95/Paper,
ISBN 0-8229-5234-3, $2.95
David P. Young, *Sweating Out the Winter*   Paper, ISBN 0-8229-5172-X,
$2.95

All prices are subject to change without notice. Order from your bookstore or
the publisher.

University of Pittsburgh Press
Pittsburgh, Pa. 15260